BELIEVE

A Catholic Lay Person's Journey
from Doubt to **Belief in
the Real Presence** of Jesus
in the Eucharist

BARBARA ARBUCKLE

Cover design: Rosemary Strohm

Printed in the United States of America
ISBN 978-1-7923-8619-0

Dedication

To Jesus who is my hope and my strength.

Acknowledgments

I am most grateful to my husband, Jim, for his constant love and support.

Before having this book published, I met with Rosemary Strohm to discuss a book on the Eucharist. I knew I chose the right person when she said, "the Eucharist is the answer to all the problems of the world." Thank you Rosemary for your wisdom and beautiful design of this book.

Sister Virginia Nolan, IHM has been my Spiritual Director since 2015. I meet with her regularly. I am extremely thankful for her immense inspiration, guidance and her gift of listening.

It has been a great blessing to have had the wisdom, inspiration and encouragement from Monsignor Ralph Chieffo, the pastor at St. Mary Magdalen Church in Media, Pennsylvania.

Arlene Finocchiaro is a dear friend of mine. She has guided me with her strong faith and knowledge which has been a great source of strength for me. Her belief in the Real Presence of Jesus in the Eucharist encouraged me to tell others. This book would not have been the same without her. I am very thankful to her and her husband Ray for editing this book.

I extend special thanks to all the witnesses who shared their statements, especially my co-adorer who walked prayerfully with me through the many beautiful experiences God has showered upon us and all that we have shared. Their names will remain anonymous.

CONTENTS

INTRODUCTION

For two thousand years, people around the world have received and continue to receive Holy Communion. Also known as the Eucharist, the word *eucharista* in the original Greek language means *thanksgiving* as those who follow Jesus rightly give thanks for this most unique of gifts.

The Catholic Church teaches something bold but extraordinary. After the priest consecrates the bread and wine, it still looks and tastes like bread and wine but, it has become the actual Body and Blood of Jesus Christ. This change of the very substance of the bread and wine is called transubstantiation and this has always been the definitive teaching of the Catholic Church.

Along with 69% of Catholics today, I believed otherwise. Due to a lack of formation or misunderstanding, I believed that the Eucharist was a mere symbol of Jesus—an act we Catholics did to simply commemorate the Last Supper. A 2019 Pew Research Center survey of US Catholics today found that most Catholics have not been properly taught the Church's teaching on transubstantiation. So, I was not alone but in the majority of what Catholics believe today. My belief changed, though, after a series of events that I believe to be supernatural.

Truth be told, I am not deserving of any special graces. Frankly, if we believe that God is all-powerful and omniscient, none of us deserve any graces. After all, we are mere finite creatures and God is infinite. But God is good and he bestows his grace to us liberally. The Church teaches that graces and blessings come freely from God when we are open to receive them. I am here to bear witness to some of these blessings I have received.

In light of the extraordinary events that I believed happened to me, one might conclude that I would see myself as particularly holy. I do not. I am no more special than anyone else! A priest once told me if someone calls you holy just tell them to be open to what God can do in your life. These words helped me since we are all granted the graces and blessings that God wants to bestow on us. We just need to keep an open heart to receive them. I do believe that, for whatever reason, God has allowed me and a few others some extraordinary graces in regards to the Eucharist.

Please go on a journey with me as I share how I went from doubt to belief that Jesus is most certainly present in the Eucharist.

CHAPTER 1

AMAZEMENT

All around the world Catholic churches have a time called Adoration. It is a time to adore Jesus. The Eucharist is held within an encasement called a monstrance. It is a sacred time to spend in prayer, praise, reflection and meditation. People bring their concerns and look to Jesus for comfort and guidance. Many come simply to adore Jesus.

I have been going to Adoration for close to six years now and go every Tuesday from noon to 1 p.m. On Tuesday, March 5, 2019, I went as usual. It was the day before Ash Wednesday. I began with a Perpetual Adoration Chaplet, a devotion that a friend gave to me. I began,

Oh my God, I believe You are truly present in the Most Blessed Sacrament.

Well, I'll stop there since I told Jesus that I could not say this part of the prayer since I did not believe that he was present in the Most Blessed Sacrament which is the Eucharist.

It is not that I don't love Jesus. I just published a book called *Allow Jesus to Love You*. It is about my love of Jesus and the desire I have for others to do the same. He knows all my sadness, my joy and my every need. I trust in him to guide and protect me from all evil. He is my Lord and Savior and my best friend.

I remember telling my own children that the Eucharist is a symbol. As a kindergarten teacher in a Catholic school, the Real Presence never came up in our training. And I don't remember it being taught in my Confraternity of Christian Doctrine classes. How was I supposed to know about the Real Presence?

After I completed the Adoration Chaplet, I was praying the rosary and went to kneel in front of the Blessed Sacrament. I saw a twig or piece of wood inside the encased Host. I thought this was unusual. Did something get caught in there? Didn't the priest notice it? There was nothing I could do about it so I continued my prayer routine.

I walked in front of the statue of Our Blessed Mother holding Baby Jesus. I often did this to ask for prayers or listen for a message. Then I heard, "Be at peace. Trust in Jesus." The statue was about six feet from where I was just kneeling and I now turned to go back to my pew. This was probably close to one minute from when I was kneeling and seeing the white Host with the twig.

I froze, seeing the Host had turned completely blood red in color. I immediately knew that this was a very holy moment. There was no doubt in my mind. I slowly moved along the pew and sat down. I felt like I was moving in slow motion. I was in complete awe of what I was seeing. I took my phone out very carefully and captured a picture from where I was sitting. The Host was bright red and emanated an extremely intense glow.

At that moment Jesus let me know he is on fire with love for us. The Host was like a burning furnace and Jesus was unable to contain himself. He was ready to explode. There was so much love coming from the Host. Internally I knew that Jesus was very sad that people do not accept his love. I had no question about the message. Suddenly a cold feeling came over me as the Host turned brown and the light no longer shown from the Host. I took another picture since the Host was now dark brown in color. I really do not have an idea of how long this took place.

Eventually the Host became white and the twig was gone.

We continued our Holy Hour of Adoration. There were four women in the chapel and three of us did see the red Host. I did not discover that only three of us saw the red Host until later in the week after sharing this event.

When our hour was over and I was outside the chapel, I asked the co-adorer if she saw the Host turn red. She did and also felt the love. I told her that Jesus showed himself and that I believe he will continue to show us more. She and I knew after sharing so many years of Adoration together through the different seasons that nothing like this ever occurred before. This was a holy moment for sure. We both felt the love pouring out from the Host. We were in awe.

Jesus knew I needed to know of his Real Presence—that he's really alive in the Eucharist. That's how much he loves me and you as well. He asks us to believe. Sometimes people need a miracle to believe. I may have needed to see with my own eyes. Saint Thomas doubted and would not believe until he saw the risen Jesus with his own eyes. He needed to touch him with his own hand. He believed once he placed

his hand into the open wound of the sacred side of Jesus.

Without a doubt, I was blinded by the light of Christ. Like Saint Paul on the road to Damascus, I was knocked off my horse and everything changed. Scripture tells us:

> On his journey, as he was nearing Damascus, a light from the sky suddenly flashed around him. He fell to the ground and heard a voice saying to him, "Saul, Saul, why are you persecuting me?" He said, "Who are you, sir?" The reply came, " I am Jesus, whom you are persecuting. Now get up and go to the city and you will be told what you must do." (Acts 9:3-6)

I did not know what was next but I felt transformed, enlightened and passionate that something must be done. Like Saint Paul, I had to wait to be told what I must do. Others must be told that Jesus is fully alive and wants a love relationship with each and every person. But how do I do this?

I went home and I showed my husband the picture of the red consecrated Host and he agreed the occurrence was something special. I was consumed with thoughts of what just occurred at Adoration and I wondered how I should handle this. So many thoughts went through my mind and my heart was on fire.

The following day I went to one of our priests and told him what happened while showing the photo. I told him of the message of Jesus on fire with love as a burning furnace. He looked closely at the photo and was in awe but was careful to not make any decision on this. I wanted everyone to know that *Jesus is alive in the Eucharist.* It was something that people needed to know. I didn't receive exact words but I know the message was that Jesus is burning with love and wants to share this love with us. Jesus wants people to know that he is suffering because people are not accepting his love.

The next day I told another priest. This time I received a very enthusiastic response confirming this is Jesus without a doubt. He was in amazement and truly believed without hesitation. He told me to be careful to whom I show this photo since some people will not believe.

The following Sunday I asked a woman who was in the chapel at the time of the red consecrated Host about her reaction. She, without doubting, saw the red Host and tried to see how the stained glass in the chapel could have made this reaction. She did not see how this came from any other source than the monstrance and shared this with the priest following Mass. She shared her words with great enthusiasm and was amazed and in awe. She believed it was a gift from the Lord.

I know that God directs and guides us. I felt a calling to check out Eucharistic miracles. I was completely overwhelmed as I watched countless videos and tried to understand transubstantiation. I researched numerous books on Eucharistic miracles and became passionate about knowing more about the Real Presence of Jesus in the Eucharist.

I have been drawn to the Sacred Heart of Jesus and chose the photo of Jesus with his Sacred Heart for the cover of my most recent book. I now believe that Jesus knew I was telling others through my writings to allow Jesus to love them and now he wanted me to feel the depth of his love. I did. Now I want others to know Jesus' intimate, overwhelming and unconditional love.

I then was inspired to read about Saint Margaret Mary Alocoque. She was mentioned while I researched books and videos. She was a French nun and mystic who died in 1690 and was canonized on May 13, 1920. She promoted devotion to the Sacred Heart of Jesus. She was so in love with Jesus when he appeared to her. She saw the burning rays of his love during Adoration. These are the words that Jesus gave to her on December 27, 1673:

> *My Divine Heart is so inflamed with love for men, and for you in particular that, being unable any longer to contain within Itself the flames of Its burning Charity, it must spread them abroad by your means, and manifest Itself to them (mankind) in order to enrich them with the precious graces of sanctification and salvation necessary to withdraw them from the abyss of perdition. I have chosen you as an abyss of unworthiness and ignorance for the accomplishment of this great design, in order that everything may be done by Me. (In Defense of the Cross, June 3, 2016)*

I clearly heard the same message that Jesus is burning with love and can no longer contain this love. This message is so important for our time. The Devotion to the Sacred Heart says it so well.

> *Jesus shows the Divine Heart as a furnace whose burning rays of love are able to reanimate faith and rekindle love in hearts grown cold and ungrateful. (Devotion to the Sacred Heart, Sisters of Mount Carmel)*

In a personal correspondence, Monsignor Ralph Chieffo confirmed my experience. "The fact that the host was on fire is a reminder that the consecrated host is still burning in love and mercy for the redemption of our souls."

When I reflect on Saint Paul's encounter with Christ, he had persecuted Christians and abruptly all that changed. Only God can change one's heart if we allow him. Saint Paul did not know what was next but followed the will of God. My heart was softened and purified by feeling the love of Jesus. My journey of believing in the Real Presence had just begun. Even though I did not know where this would lead me, I trusted that Jesus had a plan and a mission that will unfold.

WITNESS ACCOUNTS

Co-Adorer 1

On March 5, 2019, the day before Ash Wednesday, while seated in the chapel for my weekly Adoration of the Blessed Sacrament, the Host in the monstrance turned bright red. This appeared suddenly, versus a gradual reddening of the Host. Also, the redness was centered on the Blessed Sacrament (Host) itself, and not on any of the surrounding articles (e.g., altar, candles, etc.). The Host finally turned a brownish coloring; all of this took only minutes.

At that time, I had been doing weekly adoration in the Chapel for 6 years, at the same hour throughout the seasons. While lights (due to the sun and changing seasons) entered into the chapel as filtered or flowing rays during the change of seasons, this experience was unique, a one-time only event. There were no such rays of light as often occur, but a very concentrated redness on the Blessed Sacrament itself. And this phenomenon has not re-occurred in this chapel since that appearance.

On leaving the chapel, my co-adorer and I talked about this appearance and we both, separately, had felt God's absolute showing of His profound depth of love for us. It is just pouring out, and in an appearance as this, cannot be contained.

Co-Adorer 2

On Tuesday, March 5, 2019, I had a difficult situation in my life and decided to sit with Jesus in the Blessed Sacrament at Saint Maximilian Kolbe chapel around 12:00 in the afternoon.

I was amazed when I saw the monstrance holding the Blessed Consecrated Host had turned completely red. Upon looking around the chapel at the stained-glass windows, I realized that there wasn't any way the red was a reflection from the windows or anything else for that matter. A few days later, I spoke with Barbara and the other woman who regularly sat with Jesus from 12:00 to 1:00 every Tuesday and they confirmed my amazement with the red Host. Barbara asked me to go and speak to the parish priest about this occurrence. There were two priests there at the time. One of the priests expressed total belief and amazement and the other priest was skeptical. Barbara thankfully took a picture of the consecrated Host.

I believe this sighting of the red Host was a gift from God to affirm His presence in the Blessed Consecrated Host. I also felt unworthy as I was an occasional drop-in visitor to the chapel. God works in mysterious ways and I know that everyone there who witnessed this event was there for a reason beyond our own purposes for the visit.

CHAPTER 2

DISCERNMENT

The following Tuesday, March 12, I was alone at Adoration since the scheduled substitute co-adorer did not come. I was not sure what to expect and sure enough, I was amazed. The Host was full of smoke. The smoke swirled and moved with so many changes that I began taking a video to confirm this was not just my imagination. I kept a photo but later deleted the video since I questioned all of this and thought to myself, how could anyone believe this? Oh, how I wished someone was with me at this time. I was somewhat afraid since I was alone and did not understand the meaning of the smoke. It was only within the Host. There must be a significant reason for this and yet I was so unsure.

I don't know how long this occurred before I saw a large white circle at the bottom section of the Host. I overcame my fear and resolved to try and understand what I saw. Adoration continued and all was calm and peaceful.

I later showed a photo of the smoke to a friend from the church and she mentioned that around this time the Notre

Dame Cathedral was up in smoke. I checked the date and, yes, this occurred three days later.

I wondered if God was speaking through the smoke from the Host?

The word smoke is frequently referred to in the Bible.

> *Now Mt. Sinai was all in smoke because the Lord descended upon it in fire; and its smoke ascended like the smoke of a furnace, and the whole mountain quaked violently. (Exodus 19:18)*

> *And the smoke of the incense, with the prayers of the saints, ascended before God from the angel's hand. (Revelation 8:4)*

We live in such a way that we forget that the Israelites were given clear signs from God as a cloud to follow during the day and fire at night. God surely has given signs throughout history. It only takes opening the Bible to recognize that the prophets were given many signs of what was to come and to prepare. If Jesus is really present in the Host then, yes, we will be given signs. God is without limit.

In April, my co-adorer and I saw other images that were very clear. One in particular looked to be Our Blessed Mother holding Baby Jesus. She had her arm raised and I said, "She is giving Glory to God."

It may all sound like this is my imagination and I questioned and prayed that I only see what God shows me. I am thankful I was not the only one to see this. Of course, I showed it to the priest and got encouraging words of seeing this image.

Part of my discernment has been researching the miracles and keeping an open mind and heart to the supernatural and mysteries that have occurred. I found many signs or images documented in the book entitled *The Eucharistic Miracles of the World, Catalogue of the Vatican International Exhibition.*

> **Tixtla, Mexico**—October 21, 2006—"In my role as Bishop of the diocese I recognize the supernatural character of the series of events relating to the Bleeding Host of Tixtla . . . I declare the case a 'Divine Sign'." #181

> **Santarem, Portugal**—1247—The Host changed into bleeding Flesh, and Blood flowed from the Blessed Sacrament. #231

> **Bordeaux, France**—1822—In the Eucharistic miracle of Bordeaux, for more than twenty minutes, Jesus appeared in the Host exposed for public adoration, giving a blessing. #55

> **Chirattakonam, India**—2001—In the Host there appeared the face of a man similar to that of Christ crowned with thorns. #99

These images and events are only a sampling of what is documented.

In my discerning God's plan, Monsignor Ralph Chieffo's words encourage me to pursue my journey. "Fire purifies our sins and empowers us to become disciples." My response internally is yes, I want to be a disciple.

WITNESS ACCOUNT

Co-Adorer, April 16, 2019

My co-adorer and I experienced seeing a figure in the Blessed Sacrament. It appeared as a figure, holding up an arm. The figure looked like the Blessed Virgin (Mary), or Jesus Himself, but both of us saw an arm raised. I myself was so completely awed as to near tears and wondered whether the image in the Host was coming from somewhere else, possibly, one of the windows. But, no, I looked around the altar and no such images were in front or behind the monstrance or the stained-glass windows, to show this image! Again, this was a unique, isolated, one-time appearance.

I felt God again "reaching out" to us with his love and drawing us into Himself and His mercy!

CHAPTER 3

MOVED BY THE SPIRIT

Little did I know that when my husband was kind enough to take me to Canada, God had more blessings in store for me.

After receiving a brochure about a bus trip to various churches in Canada, I thought how I would love to do this. Then, around the same time, not a coincidence, I received a magazine that caught my attention. There was a photo of an old-time railroad hotel that looked like an old castle in Quebec, Canada, called the Frontenac. It was so charming and I immediately wanted to visit there. Well, this had my name on it and I told my husband that this is something that I'd really like to do. He rarely wants to travel so this was one of those times that a husband pleases his wife and makes the sacrifice. He clearly showed his desire to make this happen by going with me to the travel agency to get detailed plans, maps, hotels, etc.

He surprised me with his enthusiasm by booking tickets to a light show in the Cathedral of Notre Dame in Montreal. This was all done months in advance. We attended the light show and it was amazing and, to say the least, inspiring. Jim not being a Catholic also attended a Mass in French so you can imagine his patience at this point. I felt such a deep reverence for the Lord while meditating on the small altars within the Cathedral. You can't help but be lifted up and imagine the treasures of heaven and what God has planned for each of us.

Next, we drove to St. Joseph Oratory which is enormous. We met a Priest who blessed our marriage and lovingly spoke to us as if he was a dear friend. What a comfort when you are so far from home. It touched us to see all the crutches left at the church from people who received cures. Why do we have such a hard time believing that miracles really do happen?

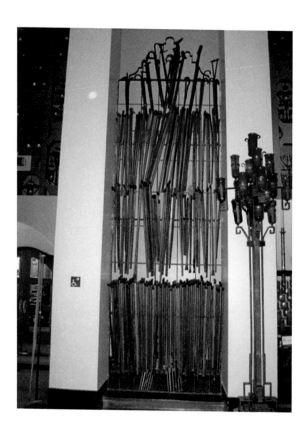

On our way to Quebec, we lost our cell phone connection after we left St. Joseph Oratory. I noticed this while Jim was driving under a tunnel. I kept quiet since I wanted to wait for a better time to break the news to Jim. I tenderly told him and we both felt lost. We do not speak French and did not understand the road signs. I then realized how much we count on our cell phones.

We stopped at a small fast-food store and Jim tried to make a computer connection. I only had US currency and wanted a bottle of water. They would not take my money. Now I was even more determined to get directions to Quebec. I went outside and asked a truck driver if he could tell us the way to Quebec. I told Jim that we have a helper so fortunately we got on the right road. After many wrong turns and much frustration, we arrived at the Frontenac in Quebec. It was more beautiful than I could have imagined. Next, we found our hotel which was within walking distance from the Frontenac.

We stayed for two days. On the first day, we took a boat ride touring the beautiful surrounding landscapes and waterfalls. The following day we went to the Citadel. Our neighbor told us to make sure that we go to the Citadel and watch the changing of the guards. The Citadel is a huge fortress that was built to protect Quebec City and the St. Lawrence River from an American invasion. It was a gorgeous summer morning and all the soldiers were in their finest uniforms. The changing of the guards occurs every day at 10 a.m. on the parade grounds. It was a remarkable experience.

We were celebrating our anniversary. We had a delightful lunch while sitting on a semi-circle sofa in the Frontenac restaurant overlooking the St. Lawrence River.

After lunch we traveled 22 miles east of Quebec City to the beautiful St. Anne de Beaupre Cathedral. It is the oldest shrine in French-speaking North America. As soon as I saw it, I was struck by its beauty and size. It was nestled in a poor community but stood out as a beacon of hope.

I drove and Jim navigated. After getting out of the car, we held hands and I thanked him for bringing me there. I was so happy. Then I stopped in front of the old chapel that was built in the 1600's. I let go of Jim's hand and said that I wanted to take this all in. I wanted to remember the people that prayed here so long ago.

Then I noticed the top of the trees on either side of the Chapel began to move rapidly, rustling, twisting and turning. It was just the leaves moving and not the whole tree. I commented that it looked like we were going to have a big storm. We continued walking several feet and then out of the right side of the wooded area came a strong driving wind that overtook us completely. It was like being in a tornado but for some reason I wasn't scared. I remember being very joyful and going along with whatever happened to me. I clearly noticed that my body was moving back and forth. I saw that my feet were still on the ground. I did not see Jim but said aloud that I think that I am going to be lifted. It was such a joy-filled experience and there was no recollection of people around me or being aware of time. As quickly as the wind came it stopped suddenly. Jim said, "**What was that**?" I told him that it was the Holy Spirit and the joy of the Blessed Mother. I was smiling and did not see him when I said this, but I remember that my arms were raised high and I was very peaceful.

The Stations of the Cross were in the hills and wooded area from which the driving wind came. The wooded area was on the right and the Cathedral was on the left of us. I marvel to this day how powerful this experience was and frequently remember this as a great comforting gift. There was a healing serenity that overcame me. I remember walking in front of the church and talking to our Blessed Mother as I looked high above the church. There was a beautiful gold statue of Saint Anne holding Mary as a child in her arms which clearly drew my attention. I was telling her of my joy in being there. The church is named after St. Anne who was the grandmother of Jesus. Jim took a photo of me on the steps and then we walked inside the church. I was very serene and wanted to focus on Jesus having a grandmother.

I sat in the back of the church and meditated on what it was like for Jesus to have a mother and grandmother to love him and wondered what were their conversations about. The mosaics were so detailed and helped me to envision the love that they shared.

I later told Jim that this was a spiritual experience. He knew it was very unusual but did not feel the same as I did but was very kind, patient and loving. After reading a reflection from the book that I happened to bring with me, it all made sense—no coincidence that this book explained my experience.

A friend had given me a book to read on the trip entitled *The Word Made Flesh* by Father Richard Veras. The following words helped me to understand that the Holy Spirit really does come to enlighten us and give us strength for the journey: *My mission is to tell others that Jesus is truly present in the Eucharist.*

In fact, Mary was there at Pentecost (Acts 1:14). She was there when the driving wind filled the house and the Holy Spirit filled the Apostles and enabled them to proclaim Jesus to the diverse crowd that had gathered. They preached without fear.

This is why Jesus tells the disciples to wait in Jerusalem until they are baptized with the Holy Spirit. (Acts 1:4-5) He does not want them to preach or heal until they are generated by his presence in the Spirit, as he is always generated by the Father in the unity of the Holy Spirit.

The teaching of the Apostles would be fruitless without the Spirit. They would just be men recounting facts of the past.

I wanted to be ready for whatever God had planned for me since I knew that I was experiencing unusual events that led me to believe I had a mission.

WITNESS ACCOUNT

James Arbuckle

We parked the car and walked, then a tremendous wind came out of nowhere prior to anything I had ever experienced in my life. It may have been one or two minutes and then it stopped as quickly as it came. Then there was a stillness in the air.

CHAPTER 4

BELIEVE

Our God is certainly a God of surprises. On October 1, 2019, I went to Adoration and near the end of the hour of prayers, praising and adoring Jesus, I was totally and completely surprised. I knelt in front of the monstrance within the main church. Most of the time, Adoration was in the chapel. While kneeling I noticed the word *Believe* on the Host. I asked my co-adorer to go to the Host and look for herself. She also saw the word *Believe*.

Then a gentleman came who began his holy hour of Adoration. I asked him to look at the Host to see if he saw the word *Believe*. He did and saw this word clearly. We agreed this was very unusual. God surely wanted this particular word to be seen. By this point, having experienced so many unusual events, I took note that this was not a mere coincidence but a clear message from Jesus.

This was not a suggestion but a request from Jesus since he will never force himself. He wants us to believe that he is really within the Host speaking to us. We all understood that we were given a glimpse into the heart of Jesus.

Now within the church high above the pews are windows with various words and flowers. The following week my co-adorer came to Adoration and she told me that she has a friend who is a scientist and her friend mentioned that if we saw a reflection of a word from the glass window it would have been in reverse as if in a mirror. I did not think of this. She later mentioned that the writing in the window was in white. Then how could we have seen this so clearly on a white host? This also did not enter into my thinking. I, of course, later questioned myself. I asked the gentleman if he saw the word *Believe* with the letters in that order. He told me, "Yes, and do not doubt yourself." This is what the evil one does to us. I agreed.

So, what are we to believe? In the book *The Eucharistic Miracles of the World* I began reading the introduction. What was the most important word? You got it—*Believe*.

> What do we believe? The simplest way to express what Christ asks us to believe about the Real Presence is that the Eucharist is really He. The Real Presence is the real Jesus. We are to believe that the Eucharist began in the womb of the Virgin Mary, that the flesh which the Son of God received from the Mother at the Incarnation is the same flesh into which He changed bread at the Last Supper, that the blood He received from His Mother is the same blood into which He changed wine at the Last Supper. Had she not given Him His flesh and blood, there could not be a Eucharist.

Faith is necessary in order to believe. I recall how Jesus sometimes could not work miracles because of the lack of faith. In every Mass, the Eucharist is a miracle. It takes faith to believe that. Sometimes even the faith of priests has been challenged.

In the above-mentioned book, a well-known miracle occurred in Lanciano, Italy in the year 750. A priest did not believe in the Real Presence of Jesus in the Eucharist. During Mass, he pronounced the words of consecration and then saw the Host turn into flesh and the wine turn into blood. This was shown to all who were present. This miracle is even more astounding because it was tested in 1971 and the "miraculous Flesh" is still intact and the "miraculous Blood" is truly blood. Please look up this for yourself. Even with this scientific proof it is only possible to accept through faith.

Jesus speaks to all of us to believe through the gospel of John:

> *I am the bread of life; whoever comes to me will never hunger, and he whoever believes in me will never thirst. But I told you that although you have seen me, you do not believe. Everything that the Father gives me will come to me, and I will not reject anyone who comes to me, because I came down from heaven not to do my own will but the will of the one who sent me, that I should not lose anything of what he gave me, but that I should raise it on the last day. For this is the will of my Father, that everyone who sees the Son and believes in him may have eternal life, and I shall raise him on the last day. (John 6:35-40)*

I choose to *Believe*! I have no doubt within me that Jesus is present in the consecrated Host. I have prayed, researched, studied miracles in detail and seen so much that the doubt is gone. Yes, it is faith that God has blessed me with. Yes, it is a gift from God. Yes, I do believe that God has much more to teach me and anyone who chooses to believe.

WITNESS ACCOUNTS

Co-Adorer 1

On October 1, 2019, while my co-adorer was praying directly in front of the Blessed Sacrament, she saw the word "Believe" in the Host. She informed me and I saw it, too. Upon leaving, we asked another co-adorer to look at the Host. Yes, he saw the word "Believe." The strange thing was, there is a stained-glass window with the word "Believe" at the back of the Church, so it was initially thought that this was a reflection of that glass "Believe" onto the Host. However, when discussing this appearance further with others, the word "Believe" on the stained-glass window is white, and so would not have transferred onto a white Host, which we saw in dark letters. Then, if the word was "reflected" onto the Host, it would have appeared backwards. So, the fact that the word "Believe" was in dark letters on a white Host, it was not a reflection from the window. What is this to us today?

Co-Adorer 2

There are moments in time when many of us experience the touch of our Lord and Savior Jesus Christ in a very special way. Recently, I encountered one of these moments while present at the Exposition of the Most Blessed Sacrament, during Adoration, at Saint Maximilian Roman Catholic Church, in West Chester, PA. An Adorer attending at this time asked me, did I see anything unusual on the "Blessed Host"?

At that time, I approached the kneeler to kneel before the monstrance containing the consecrated Host. While doing so, I saw the word "Believe" on the Host. It remained in my sight as long as I was kneeling and maintaining my focus on the Blessed Host. This was a moment of great delight, peace, and emotional joy for me.

CHAPTER 5

ANOINTED

I do believe God places people and events in our path for a particular reason. There are no coincidences. In December of 2019, I went to the store and happened to be in the same aisle as a woman who I knew for many years but rarely saw. I had taught three of her sons. She and I shared our faith and we ended up talking about our faith for close to one hour. I showed her a photo of the red consecrated Host. She wanted me to share this photo with her husband so we planned to get together at her home sometime after Christmas.

In the meantime, I mentioned that I was going to see a woman that she knew and she wanted to join me. On the day of our visit, she picked me up. It was Thursday, January 16, 2020. When we arrived at the home, I asked God to shower blessings upon this home and all who enter.

When the door opened, we were warmly greeted with hugs. We went to the kitchen and my driver and the woman we were visiting, the hostess, connected with joy and laughter. Their children were now grown and they remembered the times they shared at a Bible study when their children were young. They had lots to talk about. Her husband joined us. I asked to walk down their hallway and look at a picture that was hung on the stairway that drew my attention. It was as if Jesus called me because I truly wanted to look closely at this picture. It was of the Sacred Heart of Jesus.

Some things that occur are beyond our understanding and ability to explain so we just accept them as they are. In their home, they had a statue of Our Blessed Mother that was weeping oil. After we had time to share our faith, family connections and enjoy some food and drinks, we went into their living room where the statue was.

We looked at some of the relics and rose petals that had religious images on them. These images are a manifestation that appear on rose petals that occur at prayer services around the world. It is hard to understand how delicate images could be so precise on a rose petal but it is amazing for sure.

Some of these rose petals were placed up to a window so we could marvel at the mystery and the beauty of these images.

There was a rose petal with an image of Our Lady of Czestochowa with Saint John Paul II. The rose petal was encased in plastic and handed to me by the hostess. Holding it, I felt very quiet and listened to the conversations going on about the other relics.

The hostess said, "Look at Barbara, she has oil on her hands." I did have oil on my hands but did not understand how or why this occurred. Then she took the encased rose petal and placed it in her hand and said, "It is dry, there is no oil." Then my driver took it into her hand and said, "It is dry. This must be a gift for Barbara."

At this point I believed that if this was from God and meant for me, I wanted it all and whatever that meant, so, I placed my hands on my face. I wanted what God was giving to me.

Then I remember hearing the conversations about the relics and tried to pick up a relic of Padre Pio but dropped it. My body became very heavy and the relic was very hard to pick up.

We all sat down to pray the rosary. My body was still feeling heavy and when I went to sit, I fell back into the chair. I had two rosaries so I gave one to the woman who had driven me. The rosary began and I remember crying so hard that I was sobbing and could not speak aloud but prayed the rosary prayers in silence. I was aware of the others and when it was my turn to take the next decade I could hardly speak or catch my breath from all the tears I shed. I did whisper the next decade of the rosary and noticed the oil was still pouring out while holding the encased rose petal. My hands were covered with oil and a sweet fragrance.

When we completed the rosary, I spoke up and told them all that Our Blessed Mother is very sad. I didn't know why she was sad but it was just something that I knew and it needed to be told.

When we completed the rosary, the encased rose petal was still oozing oil. I never had any oil on my tan sweater, clothing or their chair or the rug. The hostess mentioned that she would call the woman who gave her the statue and discuss this unusual event.

My driver let me know it was time to go so I gathered my things. The hostess asked me "Did you drive?" and I told her that I did not know. Then she asked me, "Where did you park?" I said that I do not know. It was as if we were on different levels of communication.

I went to the picture of Jesus that I was drawn to when I entered their home. I needed to see it again. The image of Jesus touched me deeply. I then hugged each person and walked to the car arm-in-arm with my driver. As we were leaving, the hostess said, "Hold on to her, she may float away!"

As I stated earlier, I believe that God puts people and events in our life for a reason. My visit only confirmed that God was using me for a particular mission. The others had witnessed my anointing. This was completely unexpected and transforming for me. I was laughing and relaxed moments before the oil experience. I knew that I was given a supernatural gift. I did not try to understand all that happened to me. I wanted to be humble, obedient and open to what God had prepared for me.

WITNESS ACCOUNTS

Witness 1

I was in awe of what was happening. I was deeply moved by a very holy and intimate moment. There was so much oil on Barbara's hands. They were drenched and dripping with oil. I was concerned that the oil would go all over the rug. It did not but it stayed on her hands.

When I took the encased rose petal from Barbara the oil on it stopped. Then Barbara took it back and it wouldn't stop dripping and oozing oil. Barbara gave me a rosary while we prayed and it was saturated with oil. The oil and scent stayed with me for quite some time.

While we prayed the rosary, Barbara was between sobs and tears were flowing. She then told us that Mary was very sad. It took a while for her to recollect her thoughts. She did not know if she drove when asked. The Lord told me to protect her. I remember that seers take a long time to come back. She was deeply touched and I believe the oil was an anointing for Barbara's mission. She had a connection with Our Lady of Czestochowa since she had just visited the Pennsylvania shrine. She also has a connection with Saint John Paul II as her birthday is on his Feast Day. The rose petal that had the image of Our Lady and Saint John Paul II on it is the one that oozed the oil."

Witness 2

Barbara and another friend came to our home. From the moment Barbara entered she seemed to be being called by Jesus and His Mother. She was drawn almost immediately to an image of the Sacred Heart of Jesus we have in our foyer. She gazed at Jesus as if he were speaking to her. I was chatting with the other visitor when I saw Barbara kneeling in front of the Blessed Mother Statue we have in the living room. She told me Mary wants to touch us even when I said we should not touch the statue. We looked at some images on rose pedals that are truly gifts from Our Lady to us. I handed Barbara a rose petal encased in plastic with the image of Our Lady of Czestochowa and Saint John Paul II. As she held it, her hands became covered in oil, so much oil that it was dripping. We were in awe.

We prayed the rosary together but Barbara was crying and could hardly speak. After we finished, she was different. She had experienced something miraculous. Mary told her she was sad. Barbara felt her sadness. What a beautiful gift to be given. As my visitors left, I told Barbara to let the other visitor drive home. I thought Barbara might just float to the car. She was still in amazement.

CHAPTER 6

BLESSED

The following day after Mass, I saw the woman who drove me to the home with the Blessed Mother statue weeping oil. A visiting priest who we both knew happened to be at our church for confessions. Again, this was not a coincidence. We told him of the unusual occurrence from the previous day. I asked the priest, "What does this mean?" He said, "The oil is Jesus and let him penetrate you. Have your home blessed."

Within days, our home was blessed in a very special way called an Enthronement. Our home was consecrated to the Sacred Heart of Jesus and the Immaculate Heart of Mary.

After morning Mass, homes were being Enthroned one week following the oil experience that I had. It is quite humbling and beautiful when four or five people entered our home carrying the Our Lady of Fatima statue and singing with such joy.

They walked the grounds of our home and in every room, singing and praying. We then prayed a rosary together. I had placed a table in the center of my living room. They placed a crucifix, the statue of Our Lady of Fatima, a blessed candle and holy water on the table. There were also prayer books, blessed salt, relics and a Bible.

After we completed the rosary, I asked to have my picture taken beside the statue of Our Lady of Fatima. Take notice how the white circle appeared above the crucifix. There was a photo taken with the group in the background seconds after the first one of just me by myself. I was holding the

image of the Twin Hearts in the second photo, and the white "Host" image is not apparent.

The blessed candle that had angels engraved all over the glass holder was lit. I showed this to a priest and we believe this is the Host above the crucifix. Could Jesus present a Host wherever he wants? I try very hard not to imagine anything and trust only what God presents. God can surely do anything.

Later when I looked at the picture, I was in complete awe that Jesus would show himself in the Host in my own home, sitting on top of the crucifix. Were other people seeing this? My mind and heart were trying to comprehend the mystery of Jesus as the Host in my own home. I was trying to understand this on a human level. Was this logical?

Others confirmed what I was seeing. What was given to me was beyond my ability to explain in any scientific terms. Jesus was again giving me an experience beyond what this world could comprehend.

CHAPTER 7

ISOLATION

On March 3, 2020, I was at Adoration. Towards the end of the holy hour, I was kneeling in our church in front of the Blessed Sacrament. In the Host I clearly saw an image of a woman with a dark veil and dark dress. I saw only her profile and not her full face. She was very sorrowful and in deep prayer and leaning forward. I remember at one point her head tilted as if to acknowledge me and that she knew that I was aware of all of this. I did not look around initially to see if this was a reflection from somewhere in the church. I was in awe and kept looking since I did not know where this image was coming from and there were no images in the church that could reflect a woman in profile wearing black. I remember going back to my seat and didn't see the image. When I went back and knelt before the monstrance, I saw the same image again.

When I walked out of the church and stood in the front entrance, I told my co-adorer that I saw a lady dressed in a dark veil and dark dress. She was sad and in deep prayer. I got the chills when I told her and mentioned that I thought it was Our Blessed Mother. I left the church and started driving home. Then I made a return trip to the church to see if I imagined all of this. Well, I did not imagine this. The image was still there but very faint now. I was later reflecting on the message that I received when we completed the rosary at the home where I experienced an overflow of oil. It was without a doubt that Mary was sad.

It was March 5, 2019, when I saw the red consecrated Host. Close to one year later on March 3, 2020, I can now say without a doubt that Jesus does surely communicate through the Host.

What is this message of sadness? It is not a coincidence that at this time of Mary's sadness, the Covid 19 Virus had darkened the world. It was March 13, 2020, when former President Donald Trump declared a national emergency. Schools, businesses, sports events and mostly everything were closed or in the process of closing.

When the president shut down the country, it was ten days after I saw the sadness of Our Blessed Mother. Was the image in black a warning of things to come? Was Our Mother crying for all her children who would die alone and without the sacraments? Was she crying for her Church who for the first time in history had churches closed for Holy Week and Easter? Her son in the Eucharist—the Real Presence—was cut off from her children around the world.

Adoration stopped and there was talk of the church closing. It was all so sudden and a shock to the world. Although our church was officially closed for daily and Sunday Masses, I still went to church to pray. On an average three or four people went into the chapel or the church praying and hoping for an answer to this madness. One church in Rome had not closed for over seven hundred years and was closed on Good Friday.

Back to the question, why is Our Blessed Mother sad?

People were in isolation in nursing homes and hospitals were full of the dying. The disabled were shut in their homes. People were alone and afraid to go out. Many were turning to drugs and alcohol. Why? Fear had crippled her children. People could not receive the Bread of Life within the consecrated Host. Priests were not permitted into the hospitals to give the dying communion or hear their last confession. Priests were speaking to empty pews and zoom cameras. Those who believed in the Real Presence were starving for Jesus. Those who did not believe were hoping for an answer. Babies were not baptized and sacraments had stopped. Life had changed drastically and fear set in as to when life as we knew it could continue.

I recall the initial message of Jesus with the red consecrated Host. He is pouring out his love for us and he is very sad that we are not taking his love. Would not his mother feel the pain as well that we turned from Jesus, her son?

CHAPTER 8

BREAD OF LIFE

Jesus is reaching out to all of us in ordinary as well as extraordinary ways. We just need to keep an open heart and believe.

As I told you from the beginning, I thought communion was just a symbol. It is not. When the priest consecrates the bread and wine it becomes the Body, Blood, Soul and Divinity of Jesus.

I know this is beyond our human comprehension. It is a matter of faith and the desire to believe. This is the greatest of all the mysteries. It took an extraordinary occurrence for me to believe. Hopefully, my experience testifies as to how much Jesus wants everyone to believe that he is truly present in the Eucharist.

When I receive communion, I come as a poor sinner to receive the love and mercy that only Our Lord and Savior can give to us. I never asked for any of the favors and gifts that I have received. They were given to me. I am most grateful that Jesus showed me his Sacred Heart when I experienced the red consecrated Host. I immediately felt his love which is meant for me as well as for you.

Please allow Jesus to love you and humbly receive him in the most precious of gifts that he can give to you. He will shower you with his love and mercy. Receive him after a good confession to prepare your soul to be ready for this gift.

This journey for me has been one filled with doubt, surprises, joy, questions, research, extraordinary events and transformation.

Jesus asked Peter to walk on water and, yes, he wanted to but he was human and had his doubts. We are human and have doubts, questions and a need to see with our own eyes.

I have taken this journey with an open heart and sometimes thought I must be imagining things. I am most grateful that I have had witnesses to share and confirm these experiences. My mission is to tell others to believe in the Real Presence of Jesus in the Eucharist. He is the Bread of Life.

My hope is that you will believe what Jesus has told us in Scripture:

> *This is the bread that came down from heaven. Unlike your ancestors who ate and still died, whoever eats this bread will live forever. (John 6:58)*

REFERENCES

Scripture passages have been taken from: The New American Bible, Revised Edition. Totowa, NJ: Catholic Book Publishing Corp., 2011.

Arbuckle, Barbara. *Allow Jesus to Love You*. West Chester, PA: Self-published, 2020.

The Eucharistic Miracles of the World (Catalogue of the Vatican International Exhibition). Bardstown, KY: Eternal Life, 2009.

"Devotion to the Sacred Heart." *Sisters of Mount Carmel*. https://www.sistersofcarmel.com/devotion-to-the-sacred-heart-of-jesus.php.

"Perpetual Adoration Chaplet." *Heaven Help Us*. https://heavenhelpus.net/lets-pray.

"Sacred Heart Apparition 1673." Posted June 3, 2016. *In Defense of the Cross*. http://indefenseofthecross.com/sacred-heart-apparition/

Smith, Gregory. "Just one-third of U.S. Catholics agree with their church that Eucharist is Body, Blood of Christ." Posted August 5, 2019. *Pew Research Center* http://www.pewresearch.org/fact-tank/2019/08/05/transubstantiation-eucharist-u-s-catholics/

Veras, Richard. *The Word Made Flesh.* New York: Magnificat, 2017.

ABOUT THE AUTHOR

Barbara Arbuckle is a retired Catholic School Kindergarten Teacher. She earned her bachelor's degree in Elementary Education from West Chester University. Barbara self-published a book in 2009 entitled *Life Lessons from the Little Ones*. It is the words, wit and wisdom of the children. The children remind us of God's great love for us.

She, along with four other women, had a book published entitled *With God's Grace* in June, 2016. It is the mystery of God weaving together the lives of five strangers, and yet they share their personal healing and life-changing stories. They give glory to God for his abundant gift of grace in their lives.

Barbara had a book published entitled, *Allow Jesus to Love You* in August, 2020. She shares her love for Jesus and encourages others to know and love Jesus in a personal way.

She is a Eucharistic Minister and an Altar Server at her parish. She treasures the gift of receiving Jesus in the Eucharist as often as she can.

She lives with her husband, Jim, in West Chester, Pennsylvania, and is blessed with a son, daughter, son-in-law and three precious grandsons.